MW01065693

Manifest Power

Pew Sitter to Miracle Worker

Ed Hensel

Holy Fire Publishing
Oak Ridge, TN

Unless otherwise indicated, all Scripture quotations are taken from the New King James Version of the Bible, copyright © 1982 by Thomas Nelson, Inc., Nashville, Tennessee.

Scripture quotations marked NLT are from the *Holy Bible*, New Living Translation, copyright 1996. Used by permission of Tyndale House Publishers, Inc., Wheaton, Illinois 60189. All rights reserved.

For further information on the worldwide ministry of Holy Fire International and Evangelist Ed Hensel, contact them through:
Web site: http://www.edhensel.org
E-mail: info@edhensel.org

Copyright © 2003 November, Edward S. Hensel

All rights reserved. No part of this publication may be reproduced, stored in a retrieval system, or transmitted in any form or by any means, electronic, mechanical, photocopying, recording, or otherwise, without the prior written permission of the publisher.

Published by:
Holy Fire Publishing
P.O. Box 5192, Oak Ridge, TN 37831-5192

Edited by: Kathy Ide

Cover design by: Mrs. Vanessa R. Hensel

ISBN: 0-9745212-0-5

Printed in the United States of America and the United Kingdom

Acknowledgments

I would like to thank Dr. James T. Woodward, Sr. for his support of the ministry and his dedication to God's Word.

I would like to acknowledge apologist Kevin Birdwell for his support and dedication to Holy Fire International, and for his ongoing friendship.

Dedication

I would like to dedicate this book to my wife, Vanessa, for all of her love and understanding.

Contents

Foreword

By Dr. James T. Woodward, Sr.

Our God is a God of seasons and patterns. He moves prophetically in seasons and times. This is evidenced by the giving of the feast days to Israel, which were "appointed times"(Leviticus 23:4) . He also moved in a certain way upon the tribe of Issachar to give His people understanding of the times to know what Israel ought to do (1 Chronicles 12:32). In reading this book, Manifest Power, I am reminded that God always gives revelation before manifestation. This is a divine pattern that is given throughout the scriptures. God first tells Abraham and Sarah that they will have a son. Then He brings it to pass. He first shows Joseph that he will reign and that his family will bow down to him. Then he brings it to pass. He tells Abraham that his people will serve as slaves in captivity for 400 years and then he would bring them out. Then he brought it to pass. He speaks through the prophets that the Messiah would come. He says that he (the Messiah) would be born in Bethlehem (Micah 5:2), that he (the Messiah) would be born of a virgin (Isaiah 7:14), that he (the Messiah) would sit upon the throne of his Father David forever (Isaiah 9:7). Then He revealed that the time of the fulfillment of the promised Messiah was ready to a young virgin named Mary. When she questioned, "How shall this be seeing I know not a man?" the angel answered, "The Holy Ghost shall come upon thee, and the power of the Highest shall overshadow thee: therefore also that holy thing which shall be born of thee shall be called the Son of God." He also said that with God nothing shall be impossible. And then Mary made the confession of the ages with her own mouth she said, "Be it unto me according to thy word." (Luke 1:34-38)

This is why this book is so important to the body of Christ. It is born out of a revelation of God which gives the reader clear, concise and easy to follow explanations, directions, and principles from the Word of God of how to appropriate to the promises, the blessings, and the benefits promised by God to all his children. God wants his church to prosper and to be in health but there is a qualifying stipulation on this desire of God, He wants this to take place as our soul is prospering. (3 John 1:2)

Evangelist Ed Hensel has provided us the benefit of his experiences in foreign countries in the heat of crusade fires to stimulate the Christian to believe God for their needs and for the needs of others. He actually restates the book of Acts methodology for evangelism. He provides us with the encouragement that that we should minister as Paul the Apostle did in demonstration of the Spirit and of power. (1 Cor. 2:4) He not only reveals the Law of Faith, but he also gives clear guidance on how to cause the Law of Faith to work for you, nine guidelines for receiving a word of prophecy, along with answers to many of the questions that are baffling Christians today. It is refreshing to see a book that is simple and yet so profound.

Thank God for Evangelist Ed Hensel's gift of revelation, this is born out of Holy Ghost experience. This is the revelation that will usher in the manifestation of the restitution of all things spoken by all the holy prophets since the world began. (Acts 3:21) It will also bring about a divine reversal for the body of Christ. The reader should be mindful that this "Holy Thing" was born through the same process as Mary brought forth the physical Word of God (John 1:1-14) by the overshadowing of the Holy Ghost.

Dr. James T. Woodward, Sr.
President
Covenant Life Christian College and Theological Seminary

Introduction

Are you ready to experience the power of God in your life? Are you tired of just sitting in a pew and not seeing the power of God manifest in your life? This book will show you how to take basic biblical knowledge and bring it to manifest power. So often Christians go through life knowing that power is available and that Jesus paid the price for it all, but not sure how to access that power and see it manifest in their lives and in the people around them.

I used to live like that. Then I started to pursue the things of God in an effort to discover the secret keys that had eluded me for so long. I studied the saints of old who operated in the power of God, those who had seen unexplainable miracles and healings. I wanted to know what made them different from the average Christian today. *What makes them different from me?*

As I dug down deep in their ministries, I found that they all had different personalities and styles. Some had even made mistakes and fallen away. Yet an undeniable miraculous power inhabited their ministry.

Not long, after studying the Bible on the topic, I discovered the keys to the power of God. I started praying for deaf people, and they heard! Blind people received their sight! The lame walked and storms calmed at a single prayer.

This book is for anyone who wants to go from a pew sitter to someone who sees the power of God manifest in the physical realm. You don't have to be a scholar to understand the principles that will be brought forth in this book. You don't have to be a theologian to see the power of God manifest through your life.

This power is for today and it is here. If you're a believer in Christ, you have access to that power.

I received Jesus Christ as MY Lord and Savior in 1979, but I spent years sitting in a pew, not being used to manifest the power of God. I heard ministers and other people talk about miracles. I finally came to a point where I said, "That's it! God, I need to be fruitful in such a way that Your unmistakable power is manifested in my life." That started me on a journey to produce the manifest power of God.

CHAPTER ONE

WHAT IS MANIFEST POWER?

Simply put, manifest power is supernatural power that effects physical and emotional change. For example, a multitude near the Sea of Galilee brought to Jesus someone who was deaf and had a speech impediment, and they beseeched Him to put His hand upon this man. Jesus put His fingers into his ears, then spit and touched his tongue. Jesus then looked up to heaven and said, "Be opened." Immediately the man's ears were opened and his tongue was loosed and he spoke plainly (Mark 7:32-35).

A great windstorm arose, and the waves beat into the boat, so that it was already filling. But He was in the stern, asleep on a pillow. And they awoke Him and said to Him, "Teacher, do You not care that we are perishing?"

Then He arose and rebuked the wind, and said to the sea, "Peace, be still!" And the wind ceased and there was a great calm. But He said to them, "Why are you so fearful? How is it that you have no faith?"

Mark 4:37-40

Now that is manifest power!

Manifest power is what separates true Christianity from all other religions. Other religions have holy books bound in black leather embossed in gold with pages full of text from ancient times spanning over their religious history. So how would you convince a Hindu that Christianity is the truth and that we have the inspired Word of God? All the words in the world will not sway them.

> **MANIFEST POWER IS WHAT SEPARATES TRUE CHRISTIANITY FROM ALL OTHER RELIGIONS.**

It is when we demonstrate the Word of God in power that the miraculous happens. The apostle Paul said:

*For the kingdom of God is not in word but in **power**.*
1 Corinthians 4:20 (emphasis added)

Paul was healing the sick and touching people with the manifest power of God. This is the power of the gospel.

> *For our gospel did not come to you in word only, but also in power, and in the Holy Spirit and in much assurance.*
>
> *1 Thessalonians 1:5*

It wasn't just the apostles who were out demonstrating the manifest power of God. The Bible shows us Stephen ministering in power as well. Stephen was chosen to help the widows and distribute food, but he understood that the gospel was power for all who believe in Christ.

> *And Stephen, full of faith and power, did great wonders and signs among the people*
>
> *Acts 6:8*

What kind of power is this? The Greek word used in this passage is *dynamis*, which means miracle-working power. That power manifested in the physical realm as great signs and wonders. Stephen was a New Testament believer, just like you and me, and he had the same promises and Holy Spirit we have today. Praise God!

CHAPTER TWO

THIS POWER IS FOR YOU

This power was not just for a select few in the first century. It is for now. It is for all who believe. The Bible says in Ephesians 6:10, *"Be strong in the Lord and in the power of His might."* It was His power that raised Lazarus from the dead. It was His power that healed *"all kinds of sickness and all kinds of disease among the people"* (Matthew 4:23). Praise God, He has given us that power. Jesus said:

> *I give you the authority ... over all the power of the enemy.*
>
> Luke 10:19

We have the authority and power of Jesus Christ. If we are true believers in Christ, we are

19

joint heirs and ambassadors of Christ, with full authority to speak and act on His behalf.

The Lord uses people to carry out His will on this earth. He did it with the prophets of the Old Testament, and He is doing it now with Spirit-filled believers.

> *But you shall receive power when the Holy Spirit has come upon you: and you shall be witnesses to Me in Jerusalem, and in all Judea and Samaria, and to the end of the earth.*
>
> *Acts 1:8*

One hundred and twenty believers received the power of the Holy Spirit on the Day of Pentecost. And we serve a God who changes not. The disciples of Christ today are empowered to preach the gospel, heal the sick, cleanse the lepers, raise the dead, and cast out demons (Matthew 10:7-8).

Jesus said in John 8:31, *"If you abide in My word, you are My disciples indeed. And you shall know the truth, and the truth shall make you free."* Every believer who abides in the Word is a disciple of Christ. If you are a Bible-believing Christian, this power is for you.

In the gospel of John, we find Jesus speaking to believers. He states:

> *Most assuredly, I say to you, he who believes in*

Me, the works that I do he will do also; and greater works than these he will do, because I go to My Father."

John 14:12

Jesus is speaking to "he who believes in Me." If you are a believer in Jesus Christ, this is addressed to you. Jesus wants *you* to do the same works He did. He healed the sick, raised the dead, cleansed the leapers, and performed many other mighty miracles. My friend, he wants you to do all that "and greater works."

I have heard it preached that salvation is the "greater work." I agree. So the lesser works, like physical healing and deliverance, should be easy.

The next verse says:

And whatever you ask in My name, that I will do, that the Father may be glorified in the Son.

John 14:13

If we ask for something so that the Father may be glorified in the Son, He will do it. That will bring manifest power.

I had the privilege of preaching in southern India recently, where we rented a hall that was normally used for wedding ceremonies. We invited the Hindus and Muslims to come and hear the gospel. We passed out flyers and put up posters inviting people to come to hear and see the power

21

of God.

On the first night, there were about 250 people assembled. All were unbelievers except the ministry workers. I stood in front of those people and preached the simple truth of the gospel. I told them about Jesus' love for them. I told them that Jesus died for their sins, and by His stripes they were healed, and that God wanted to have a personal relationship with them.

After I was finished speaking my fifteen-minute message, I told the crowd I would prove to them that Jesus Christ is alive. I asked if anyone there was deaf. A man in the back of the room signaled that he had been deaf in his right ear for the last twelve years.

This man hadn't intended to come to the meeting to hear the gospel. He simply worked at the hall as the watchman.

After two ushers assured him that we were not going to harm him in any way, he came forward and stood on the platform. I asked him, "Sir, is it true that you're deaf in your right ear?"

"Yes," he said.

I turned to the crowd. "In order that the Father may be glorified in the Son, and so that you will know that Jesus Christ is alive today and risen from the dead, God will heal this man on the platform in front of your very eyes."

The assembled crowd got quiet. I stood there, knowing that my Lord was going to heal this

Faith

man. I laid my hands on his deaf ear and prayed:

Lord, in the name of Your Son, Jesus Christ, open this deaf ear so all will know Jesus as Lord. Forget not Your Word, Father, and be glorified in Your Son, Jesus, as this man will be a living testimony of Your manifest power. I rebuke the deaf spirit and command it to come out now. By the name, power, and blood of Jesus. Amen.

Those Hindus and Muslims waited attentively to see what the deaf man would do.

Finally, he said, "I can hear little bit, but not everything."

I looked him in the eyes and said, "You will be completely healed right now in the name of Jesus."

> **WHEN PEOPLE OF OTHER FAITHS SEE THAT THE GOD WE SERVE IS NOT JUST IN WORD ONLY, BUT IN MANIFEST POWER, THEY BELIEVE.**

Immediately his ear opened. He could hear the slightest whisper. The man was so excited! He had become a living testimony to the manifest power of Jesus Christ.

I turned to the crowd of Hindus and Muslims. "Is there anyone here who would like to receive Jesus Christ as his Lord and Savior? Jesus is alive and risen from the dead. Only the Lord can open the ears of a deaf man. I have proven to you this day that my God is the true God.

Almost every single person in that room came forward to accept Jesus Christ as Lord and Savior. Praise the Lord!

When people of other faiths see that the God we serve is not just in word only, but in manifest power, they believe. Jesus said:

"Believe Me that I am in the Father and the Father in Me, or else believe Me for the sake of the works themselves."

John 14:11

What works is Jesus talking about in this verse? He is talking about those works that bring forth the physical manifestation of the power of the Holy Spirit.

Can you say to an unbeliever, "Believe me that Jesus Christ is Lord. And if you don't believe me, believe for the sake of the works that Jesus does through me because the kingdom of God is not in word but in power"? Deaf men can hear because of the power of Jesus. Paralytics can walk because of Jesus. To Him be all the glory!

There are several keys you will learn through this book that will help you step out and see the manifest power of God in your life and in the lives of others. In these last days we need to spread the gospel with conviction and power. The

24

hurting world needs a touch from the living Savior. You and I hold the good news, so let's go out and do the work of the Lord in manifest power!

CHAPTER THREE

WHAT IS THE POWER FOR?

I think it is important to discuss why we would pursue the power of God, because if we act with the wrong motives, this power will not manifest.

God gives us power so we can touch people's lives where they are hurting. The most important thing we can do as believers in Jesus Christ is to win the lost. The only things you can take with you to heaven are those people you've been able to witness to.

We need to have a burden for the lost. God has chosen us to be ambassadors of the kingdom of heaven while we're on the earth. We represent Jesus Christ. He has chosen us to preach the good news. Praise God, He has equipped us with the manifest power of His presence.

In Matthew 10:7-8 we read:

And as you go, preach, saying, "The kingdom of heaven is at hand." Heal the sick, cleanse the lepers, raise the dead, cast out demons. Freely you have received, freely give.

Throughout Scripture we see this pattern. God tells us that we should preach or teach first, then heal the sick, cleanse the lepers, raise the dead, and cast out demons. In Matthew alone we find lots of places where Jesus preached and taught the gospel before He performed the miraculous.

> **GOD GIVES US POWER SO WE CAN TOUCH PEOPLE'S LIVES WHERE THEY ARE HURTING.**

Then Jesus went about all the cities and villages, teaching in their synagogues, preaching the gospel of the kingdom, and healing every sickness and every disease among the people.

Matthew 9:35

And Jesus went about all Galilee, teaching in their synagogues, preaching the gospel of the kingdom, and healing all kinds of sickness and all kinds of disease among the people. Then His fame went through-

28

*out all Syria; and they brought to Him all sick people
who were afflicted with various diseases and torments,
and those who were demon-possessed, epileptics, and
paralytics; and He healed them*

Matthew 4:23-24

Jesus was clearly showing a pattern for ministry. First we preach the Word because faith comes by hearing, and hearing by the Word of God (Romans 10:17). God gives us power not because of who we are, but to show us who He is. Therefore we have confidence not in ourselves, but in Christ, who will never forsake us.

This takes the pressure off of us. When we obediently preach or teach the Word of God, we can be assured that God's Word will not return void. The manifest presence of God is in our lives to confirm the Word

> **THE MANIFEST PRESENCE OF GOD IS IN OUR LIVES TO CONFIRM THE WORD OF GOD AND BRING GLORY TO THE FATHER THROUGH HIS SON, JESUS CHRIST.**

of God and bring glory to the Father through His Son, Jesus Christ.

Many of you who have heard me proclaim the gospel and minister the manifest power of God have heard me say, "So that the Father may be glorified in the Son, and so that all will know that Jesus is risen from the dead, Lord, perform this miracle." I give Jesus all the glory, honor, and praise because He is the one who paid the price. He has performed every miraculous thing that happens through me in our gospel meetings.

CHAPTER FOUR

AMBASSADORS FOR CHRIST

Knowing who you are in Christ is one of the most important keys in seeing the manifest power of God. In our society today it is harder than ever to see ourselves as God sees us. When we don't see ourselves as He does, and we see ourselves defeated and worthless it directly impacts how we see God.

If we don't see ourselves as God sees us, we will not be able to minister boldly by allowing the Holy Spirit to use us they way He wants to.

In 2 Corinthians 5:20 we read:

Now then, we are ambassadors for Christ, as though God were pleading through us: we implore you on Christ's behalf, be reconciled to God.

What does it mean to be an ambassador? If you were an ambassador for the United States to Uganda, you would be responsible for representing your country. You would have all the authority that the president of the United States gives you. You could even legally bind the United States in an agreement that would have to be honored.

> **JESUS HAS GIVEN US AUTHORITY OVER ALL THE POWER OF THE DEVIL.**

You would also be responsible for the citizens of your country in that nation, helping them and assisting those in trouble.

We are Christ's ambassadors on the earth, representing the kingdom of God. With the title of Ambassador for Christ comes authority.   Jesus clearly described what authority we have:

Behold, I give you authority ... over all the power of the enemy.

power

Luke 10:19

Wow! Jesus has given us authority over all the power of the devil. So often Christians run around acting victimized, as if they were under the devil's foot and he was about to snap their neck. Satan does not have power over a believer in Jesus

32

(unless the believer gives it to him.) Exercise your authority as an ambassador for Christ. Don't be victimized any longer. Realize who you are in Christ.

Jesus went on to say:

Assuredly, I say to you, whatever you bind on earth will be bound in heaven, and whatever you loose on earth will be loosed in heaven.

Matthew 18:18

Notice that word <u>assuredly</u>. That means without a doubt, clear cut, you can bank on it, it will definitely happen. Whatever we loose or bind on earth will be loosed or bound in heaven. That is authority we can act on as ambassadors for Christ.

For example, you can pray, "I bind that deaf spirit and cast it out and loose healing power to your ear in the

> **THE RIGHTEOUSNESS OF GOD IS FOR ALL WHO PUT THEIR FAITH IN JESUS.**

name of Jesus." You have the authority to say that to a deaf person and expect him to hear. Not because of who you are, but because of who you represent: Jesus Christ.

Christ confirms this over and over in Scripture. He said, "These signs will follow those who believe: In My name they will cast out demons

33

. . . they will lay hands on the sick, and they will recover" (Mark 16:17-18).

We are the righteousness of God in Jesus. That means we are in right standing with God. If we are believers, he no longer sees our sin. We are fully reconciled to Him.

For He made Him who knew no sin to be sin for us, that we might become the righteousness of God in Him.

2 Corinthians 5:21

Do you see yourself as the righteousness of God? Many in the church today are saying, "I am nothing but a wretched sinner who asked Jesus into my heart. "

> **SEEING YOURSELF AS GOD SEES YOU WILL MAKE IT EASIER FOR YOU TO MINISTER IN POWER BY FAITH.**

My friend, you are a lot more than that. You are righteous through Christ. Believe it. Start seeing yourself as God sees you. God is speaking to those Christians who feel as if they're no good. He is saying:

I have already paid the price.
I give you authority over the devil.
You are redeemed.

34

You are no longer condemned.
You are the righteousness of God.
You are My ambassador.
Nothing is impossible through Me.

If you're a Christian, you are in good standing with God because Jesus paid the price by dying on the cross. This righteousness of God is for all who put their faith in Jesus.

... even the righteousness of God, through faith in Jesus Christ, to all and on all who believe. For there is no difference; for all have sinned and fall short of the glory of God, being justified freely by His grace through the redemption that is in Christ Jesus, whom God set forth as a propitiation by His blood, through faith, to demonstrate His righteousness, because in His forbearance God had passed over the sins that were previously committed, to demonstrate at the present time His righteousness, that He might be just and the justifier of the one who has faith in Jesus.

Romans 3:22

Seeing yourself as God sees you will make it easier for you to minister in power by faith. Some people believe if you pay enough money to the church, you might be able to convince God to give you a trickle of His power. My friend, Christ's sacrifice on the cross was enough. If you are a believer in Christ, you have the power and authority

35

because Jesus has given it to you.

On a recent trip to Africa, I was preaching at an outdoor evangelistic crusade where thousands of people were gathered to hear the gospel preached. A wooden platform had been constructed in an open field. The only power we had came from generators behind the platform. I could hear them humming in the background as they powered the sound system and lights. The lights consisted of exposed glass bulbs strung together with loose wiring.

Just as I stepped up to the podium to preach, a drop of rain hit my Bible. Looking up at the night sky, I couldn't even see one star. The wind started to pick up. But I was determined that no amount rain or wind would stop me from preaching.

I had barely gotten started when a downpour started. That was fine with me because I was on a mission. But a lot of the people were running for cover. As those cold raindrops started hitting the hot, exposed light bulbs, they started bursting.

I knew it was the will of God for the gospel to be preached to those people. Many needed salvation, healing, and deliverance. So I stretched forth my hands and prayed:

"In the name of Jesus, I command this rain to stop so that the gospel can be preached and so that the Father may be glorified in the Son."

Within two minutes the clouds parted, the stars started showing through, and the rain stopped. The ministry coordinator stood before the crowd and said, "The man of God has prayed and the rain has stopped. Come and take your place."

It was a miracle! It was the manifest power of God. I was an ambassador of Christ, justified and righteous in his sight. God is the one who stopped the rain, but I had faith to believe because I knew who I was in Christ!

Many Christians today do not believe they are ambassadors of Christ to bring the manifest power of God. They seem to act as if Jesus' death, burial, and resurrection were not enough. Not only did Jesus pay the price, He gave us authority and recorded in His Word so all will know that they can minister in manifest power.

CHAPTER FIVE

THE LAW OF FAITH REVEALED

The Law of Faith is one the fundamental keys to bringing about the power of God in the physical realm. We will be looking at four core elements in the Law of Faith and how to apply them to see the miraculous.

You can walk in the fullness of what God has called you to; for example, healing the sick, raising the dead, cleansing leapers, casting out demons, and speaking the Word boldly with signs and wonders.

We read in Hebrews 11:6, "Without faith it is impossible to please Him." This verse clearly states that we need faith. Romans 3:28 says, "We conclude that a man is justified by faith." Many people think that faith is an unobtainable mystery. I am sure you have heard people say, "I guess I just don't have enough faith," or "I am not at that level," as if there were some sacrifice they needed to make or that God didn't want them to obtain a deeper level of faith.

Some church leaders have made things worse by complicating the issue. They outline complex levels of anointing in the New Testament church that can only be obtained through rigorous fasting and pleading with God, as if God were holding something back. The gospel is simple and God wants you to understand it.

Remember the day you got saved? Weren't you amazed at how simple it was to become a believer? It was a free gift, and all of your good works meant nothing.

> **THE FAITH IT TOOK TO BE SAVED IS THE SAME FAITH IT TAKES TO BE USED POWERFULLY BY GOD.**

The only thing that mattered was the finished work of Jesus Christ on the cross! Do you remember how the burdens were lifted from your heart when you knew that Jesus saved you?

The faith it took to be saved is the same faith it takes to be used powerfully by God.

Faith is so simple! It just means believing that you are who God says you are and that you can do what He says you can do. He wants you to have great faith and to be a powerful Christian.

The problem is, many people don't understand the basic truths that God defines in His Word.

Whenever you have read about great men or women of faith in the past, have you said to yourself, *That person has a special anointing. How can I be like them? What makes their prayers work?* I have asked those questions myself in years past. If you grab hold of the principles in this book, your whole life will change. That is what has happened for thousands of others who have realized the truth that is presented here.

The Law of Faith is more than just a theory. It is fact. The Bible is clear on the principles that bring about the miraculous. God's Word will not return void, so when you exercise the Law of Faith, it always produces results!

The Law of Faith consists of four basic elements:

1. Recognizing the Word
2. Proclaiming the Word
3. Demonstrating the Word
4. Receiving the Results

Often our faith is determined by some experience or person we know rather than these four elements, so the outcome is less than consistent or maybe nonexistent. For example, you hear someone say that his grandmother was a woman of God with faith, but she died of cancer so her prayers must not have worked. This experience makes it difficult to have faith in God for the miraculous.

God's Word is true and infallible.   He will never fail you. If you have the faith of a mustard seed, nothing will be impossible for you (Matthew 17:20).   We need to evaluate our faith and see if it lines up with the Law of Faith as it is presented in the Word of God instead of matching it up against our own ideas of what we think faith is.

You believe that there is one God. You do well. Even the demons believe — and tremble! But do you want to know, O foolish man, that faith without works is dead?

James 2:19-20

Just believing that God exists, or even knowing it in your head, is not the living faith we read about in the book of James. The disciple is talking here about a faith that produces works and manifests power!

We read in John 14:12:

Most assuredly, I say to you, he who believes in Me, the works that I do he will do also; and greater works than these he will do, because I go to My Father.

There is that word *assuredly* again.
In this passage we find a promise of Jesus

that will stand against any obstacle. This passage applies to "he who believes in me." Praise God, that is any believer today.

Jesus says that believers will do the same kind of works that He did. What work did Jesus do?

The Bible tells us what happened when John the Baptist heard about the works of Jesus.

And when John had heard in prison about the **works of Christ***, he sent two of his disciples and said to Him, "Are You the Coming One, or do we look for another?"*

Jesus answered and said to them, "Go and tell John the things which **you hear and see***: The blind see and the lame walk; the lepers are cleansed and the deaf hear; the dead are raised up and the poor have the gospel preached to them. And blessed is he who is not offended because of Me."*

2-5

Matthew 11:4-11 (emphasis added)

Luke 7: 18-23

John the Baptist wanted to find out if Jesus was the savior. Jesus didn't just say, "Yes, I am the one." He told John and his followers about the manifest power demonstrated in His life. The blind were seeing, deaf were hearing, lame were walking, lepers were cleansed, and the dead were raised. Praise God!

Then Jesus made a powerful statement. "Who ever believes in Me" will do the same works that He did. (John 14:12) Do you believe that? It is time for you to step into the fullness of what God has called you to do as a believer. God wouldn't say you could do the works if He didn't enable you to.

I want to take a moment at this point and make it clear that I am not talking about works for salvation. Only by grace through faith are you saved and in the family of God. Romans 10:9-10 makes it clear that if we confess our sins and believe in our hearts that God has raised Jesus from the dead, we will be saved.

It is God's desire that we, as children of His, produce good fruit and perform works so that the Father may be glorified. We need to start using our faith to bring about the manifest power of God!

But be doers of the word, and not hearers only, deceiving yourselves.

James 1:20

James makes it clear that we should be out doing the Word of God. That means performing the same works Jesus Christ did. For those who believe, nothing is impossible.

CHAPTER SIX

RECOGNIZING THE WORD

"Recognizing the word" is the first element in the law of faith. It must be the first thing we seek before seeing the manifested result. God's Word is final and it brings the power. ☆

The Bible is inspired and infallible. Praise God! We can count on it. We can know that it is truth and fact. If we believe that, we will act upon it, and then we will see results.

By the word of the Lord the heavens were made, and all the host of them by the breath of His mouth.

Psalm 33:6

The Word of God stands above all else. Everything that exists was created by God's word.

God's words caused the universe to come into existence. He has chosen words to be containers of power!

> **WHEN WE TAKE THE LIVING WORD, JESUS CHRIST, AND PROCLAIM HIM TO THE WORLD, MIRACULOUS THINGS HAPPEN.**

For with God nothing is ever impossible, and no word from God shall be without power or impossible of fulfillment.

Luke 1:37 (AMP)

If we realized how powerful the words of Scripture are, we wouldn't just carry a Bible with us to church because that is what everyone expects of us. We would study God's Word, read it often, and do whatever it says.

For the word of God is living and powerful, and sharper than any two-edged sword, piercing even to the division of soul and spirit, and of joints and marrow, and is a discerner of the thoughts and intents of the heart.

Hebrews 4:12

His Word can bring life to your Christian walk. But if you don't know what the Bible says, how can you act on it?

46

It is the Spirit who gives life; the flesh profits nothing. The words that I speak to you are spirit, and they are life.

John 6:63

Some say that the miracles in the Bible have passed or that the words God spoke in the Scriptures were for someone else. I declare to you that God does not change (Malachi 3:6). His words shall never pass away (Matthew 24:35). Praise God! He is the same yesterday, today, and forever (Hebrews 13:8).

God has given us the authority to use His living and powerful words. The problem is, many of us don't know what those words are.

For years, I attended church three times a week, read my Bible occasionally, and prayed, but most of what I knew was only surface deep. The majority of the knowledge I had was gleaned from thirty- to sixty-minute messages on Sunday mornings.

For example, I believed that God healed people physically, but I wasn't sure if it was His will to heal everyone, and I didn't believe that I could be used to pray for others to be healed.

Before I could operate in the manifest power of healing, I had to know what the Scriptures have to say about the subject. I also needed to know the will of God on the matter. Since Jesus never changes and the words of Scripture are living and powerful, I knew I could trust what I studied from the Bible.

After I studied the verses on healing and knew what the will of God was on the matter based on the written Word of God. I applied the four elements of faith: Recognizing the Word, proclaiming the Word, demonstrating the Word and receiving the results. Then the manifestations came. The lame were walking and the deaf were hearing. Miracles followed me everywhere I went. Praise God!

I give all the glory and honor to Jesus Christ because He alone deserves the praise. I am just thankful He has chosen people to manifest His power in order to touch others who are hurting.

There was a man at one of our meetings who had been unable to walk for over a decade. His bones had grown stiff and he was unable to bend his legs. When I preached the gospel that day, he was so touched he asked people to help him forward so he could accept Jesus Christ as his Savior. He prayed the sinner's prayer and then asked me to pray for him to be healed.

I anointed him with oil and prayed the prayer of faith. At first, nothing happened physically. He still couldn't walk. I told him, "You are healed so that all will know that Jesus is alive. You are healed as a living testimony of Jesus Christ." After I said that, I moved on because there were several thousand people at the meeting with a lot of

(needs.)

The following night, the man came forward again. With tears running down his face he said, "After I went to sleep last night, something lifted me from my bed and bent my legs. When I woke up this morning, I was completely healed and able to walk!"

Hallelujah! I knew God's Word would not return void. It was glorious to see how God touched this man. All who knew Him were amazed. We serve an awesome God!

> **ONCE WE RECOGNIZE THE POWER OF THE WORD OF GOD IN OUR LIVES, WE WILL BE ABLE TO PROCLAIM THAT WORD AND DEMONSTRATE THAT IT BRINGS LIFE TO ALL WHO ACCEPT IT.**

In the beginning was the Word, and the Word was with God, and the Word was God. He was in the beginning with God. All things were made through Him, and without Him nothing was made that was made. In Him was life, and the life was the light of men. And the light shines in the darkness, and the darkness did not comprehend it.

John 1:1-5

When we proclaim the gospel of Jesus Christ, we are proclaiming the Word that does not change. We are proclaiming the life and light of men. Hallelujah! Jesus did not come to condemn the world but to save it.

It is time for us to recognize the Word of God as the authority in our lives. When we take the living Word, Jesus Christ, and proclaim Him to the world, miraculous things happen.

> *For this reason we also constantly thank God that when you received the word of God which you heard from us, you accepted it not as the word of men, but for what it really is, the word of God, which also performs its work in you who believe.*
>
> *1 Thessalonians 2:13*

Once we recognize the power of the Word of God in our lives, we will be able to proclaim that Word and demonstrate that it brings life to all who accept it.

Abraham had great faith. He recognized God's promise.

> *He did not waver at the promise of God through unbelief, but was strengthened in faith, giving glory to God, and being fully convinced that what He had promised He was also able to perform. ? And therefore "it was accounted to him for righteousness."*
>
> *Now it was not written for his sake alone that it was imputed to him, but also for us. It shall be imputed to us who believe in Him who raised up Jesus*

our Lord from the dead, who was delivered up because of our offenses, and was raised because of our justification.

Romans 4:20-25

We can trust in the Word of God and His promises. They are for all who believe in Jesus.

The words of God come in different forms.

God can speak to us in many different ways. He speaks through His written Word, the spoken word (preaching and prophecy), and directly to our spirits.

First and foremost the Bible is the infallible Word of God. It is powerful and living. We should do nothing contrary to God's written Word. It is the final authority on any topic. That is why we need to study the Scriptures.

All Scripture is given by inspiration of God, and is profitable for doctrine, for reproof, for correction, for instruction in righteousness, that the man of God may be complete, thoroughly equipped for every good work.

Timothy 3:15

When we hear the Word of God spoken by a preacher or teacher, we should receive these words as from the Lord. However, we must examine what we hear from people by verifying their words with

(the written Word.)

I was talking to a minister recently who has been in the ministry for thirty years. We were discussing an issue, and he was convinced he knew the will of God on the matter. However, after I showed him some Scriptures, he decided to research the issue further and pray about it. Several months later he came to me and said, "I have been taught wrong." He had assumed something based on what he had been taught in his denomination.

The written Word of God is the final authority on every topic. We should receive preaching and teaching, but we should always compare it to the Bible and keep that which matches up and reject what does not.

God also speaks directly to our spirits. For example, during your daily prayer time you may be overwhelmed with a thought and you sense in your spirit it is from God. When God speaks to us like that, it is usually regarding something specific in our lives.

I have heard people say, "God told me this" when it is obvious they simply want to get some kind of selfish motive fulfilled. If God is truly speaking to you, His voice will bear witness to your spirit and you will know God is truly speaking. God will never ask you to do something that is contrary to His written Word.

I receive invitations to speak in many different countries around the world. Often, when I am praying about the next country I should go to and preach the gospel, God will speak to me and I'll know which direction to go.

After my time in prayer, if I sit still and listen, I will hear His quiet voice. I encourage you to do the same. You will be amazed at what God will speak to your spirit.

Prophecy and the Word of God

Prophecy is another way we hear God's word.

And so we have the prophetic word confirmed, which you do well to heed as a light that shines in a dark place, until the day dawns and the morning star rises in your hearts; knowing this first, that no prophecy of Scripture is of any private interpretation, for prophecy never came by the will of man, but holy men of God spoke as they were moved by the Holy Spirit.

But there were also false prophets among the people, even as there will be false teachers among you, who will secretly bring in destructive heresies, even denying the Lord who bought them, and bring on themselves swift destruction. And many will follow their destructive ways, because of whom the way of truth will be blasphemed. By covetousness they will exploit you with deceptive words; for a long time their

53

judgment has not been idle, and their destruction does not slumber.

2 Peter 1:19–2:3

We must be careful when receiving a word of prophecy. We need to confirm the prophetic word as the Scripture indicates. Since a lot of people are misled in this area, here are nine guidelines for receiving a prophetic word.

1. Test Everything

First Thessalonians 5:21 tells us that we should test everything and hold fast to that which is good. If someone gives you a prophecy, test it by comparing it with Scripture. If it doesn't hold water, discard the so-called prophetic word.

2. Don't put your own interpretation on a prophetic word.

So often, when we receive a word of prophecy, we try to make it fit into our own interpretation or understanding. This can be dangerous. If the word is prophetic, its meaning will come to light.

3. Don't reject a surprising word out of hand.

Sometime a word will come that is totally unexpected, about something you have never thought of. Don't discard it. If that word is of

God, it will be confirmed.

4. Don't try to make a prophetic word come to pass.

God does not intend for you to force something to happen. Let's say someone came to you and said, "God told me that you will write a book." That doesn't mean you should start writing today, or that you should write on whatever topic you were thinking about at that moment. The prophetic word may be for five years from now. If you tried to make a prophetic word like that happen, you could end up with a garage full of books you can't sell.

5. Never make a decision on a prophetic word alone.

The prophetic word must be confirmed. Let's say someone came to you and said, "Thus saith the Lord: You are to become a full-time missionary to Bolivia." Does this mean you should sell everything you own and move? Not necessarily. On the other hand, if God has been dealing with you for months about going to Bolivia and being a full-time missionary, and someone who doesn't know you gives you a prophetic word, then it may very well be a confirmation.

6. Don't move without a confirmation.

I have known people who received a prophecy and acted on it without a confirmation, only to find out they were being led astray.

7. Don't let anyone put you into bondage.

If someone says I have a word of the Lord for you, and that word puts you into bondage, it is not from the Lord. Never receive a prophetic word that has no way of glorifying God.

I have a Christian friend who went to a cell group where a man prophesied that she had a spirit of witchcraft and that she would be bound by it. Obviously this man is a false prophet, because Jesus sets people free. Besides, my friend was a good Christian and had never been involved in witchcraft.

8. Don't seek out prophetic words.

We shouldn't be running around trying to find someone to prophecy over us. If God wants to give you a word by way of prophecy, He will do so. Prophecy is not a fortune-teller scenario. If you are a child of God, you have the same access to the Lord as anyone else. You don't have to seek out prophets to get a word from God.

9. Don't accept a word outside of accountability.

If the person giving the prophecy is a true

prophet, he or she will be accountable in the local church. The church leadership will vouch for that person and tell you whether or not this is a man or woman of God. You may find out that the person who gave the prophecy has a track record for leading people astray.

We should not despise prophecy and we should desire gifts of the spirit. In First Corinthians 14:1 Paul states:

Pursue love, and desire spiritual gifts, but especially that you may prophesy.

Recognizing the Word is a very important element in the law of faith. Without this element you will be a ship lost at sea with no compass not knowing what direction to go. However once you recognize what God is saying to you go out with all your might to accomplish His will in you life.

CHAPTER

SEVEN

PROCLAIMING THE WORD

The four elements in the law of faith are recognizing the Word, proclaiming the Word, demonstrating the Word, and receiving the results. In this chapter we will study the second element in the law of faith. Once we know what God's Word is, we must proclaim it. This is the way God has designed faith to work. God show us by example. God spoke words and the manifestations of His words to came to pass.

If you speak the written Word of God, those are containers for power! Jesus demonstrated this to us.

Then Jesus was led up by the Spirit into the wilderness to be tempted by the devil. And when He had fasted forty days and forty nights, afterward He was hungry. Now when the tempter came to Him, he said, "If You are the Son of God, command that these stones become bread."

But He answered and said, "It is written, 'Man shall not live by bread alone, but by every word that proceeds from the mouth of God.'"

Matthew 4:1-4

When He was tempted, Jesus quoted Scripture. He said, "It is written." Jesus showed us that the words of scripture have power.

When He was tempted by the devil, Jesus spoke. We need to speak out the Word of God in faith.

*So Jesus answered and said to them, "Have faith in God. For assuredly, I **say** to you, whoever **says** to this mountain, 'Be removed and be cast into the sea,' and does not doubt in his heart, but believes that those things he **says** will be done, he will have whatever he **says**. Therefore I **say** to you, whatever things you ask when you pray, believe that you receive them, and you will have them.*

Mark 11:22-24 (emphasis added)

Whoever "says," and believes the things he "says," will have what he "says." Jesus is clearly showing us the power of the proclaimed word. That's why we can say, "By His stripes we were healed" (1 Peter 2:24).   I WAS

In a recent meeting, while I was preaching the gospel, I told the crowd that if they were blind they would see, and if the were deaf they would hear, and if they were lame they could walk, if they would put their faith in Jesus.

I proclaimed words of power in that place. When I gave an altar call for salvation, about 200 people came forward. One of them was a teenage boy who was clinically blind. He wanted to accept Jesus as his Savior.

After the salvation prayer I made a corporate prayer for healing, proclaiming the Word of God over these new believers in Christ. Instantly the boy said he could see, but his eyes felt like they were on fire. He stayed in that condition until the next night, when he came forward for more prayer.

> **YOU CAN BE SURE THAT THE POWER WILL MANIFEST...SO THE FATHER MAY BE GLORIFIED IN THE PERFORMING OF HIS WORD THAT IS IN YOUR HEART.**

He figured if God could give him his sight, He could also take away the burning feeling in his eyes. In the corporate prayer that night, that boy was fully healed. He came forward and testified to the miraculous power of Jesus.

The Word of God has power. No one laid hands on that boy. He was healed solely by Jesus, through the power of His Word.

We must boldly proclaim the Word and believe that God will perform it because He is faithful.

> *If you abide in Me, and My words abide in you, you will ask what you desire, and it shall be done for you. By this My Father is glorified, that you bear much fruit; so you will be My disciples.*
>
> *John 5:7*

Jesus is saying, "If you abide in Me" (if you are a saved, born-again, Bible-believing Christian) and "My words abide in you" (which is the first element in the law of faith), then you can expect miraculous things to happen.

You can ask whatever you desire, and it shall be done for you. But we must speak it out loud. This is the second element of faith.

Now, does this mean if you want a Lexus, all you have to do is speak it out and you will soon be driving a Lexus? Of course not. We are not told to claim whatever our flesh desires. God is not interested in satisfying your flesh. His words, which abide in you, will be done.

If you understand His Word on healing, you will be healed or be used in healing. If you understand what the Word says about a believer's ability to cast out devils, you will be a deliverer because God's Word says, "It shall be done for you." Hallelujah! The power will manifest when you minister the Word of God to someone who is hurting.

You can be sure that the power will manifest. Not so you can show off a Lexus to your friends, but so the Father may be glorified in the performing of His Word that is in your heart. That is why I say, "So that the Father may be glorified in the Son, you are healed and delivered."

CHAPTER EIGHT

DEMONSTRATING THE WORD

Not only do we need to realize the Word and speak the Word, it is essential that we put action to the Word.

If you believe something, you should act like you believe it. Otherwise you are just paying lip service to it. For example, before you sit in a chair, you must believe it will hold your weight. If not, you won't sit in it. You act on the belief that it will hold you.

Let's say you go to a fast-food restaurant and order a hamburger. The person taking your order tells you it will cost $2.99. So you give him your money. You believe that if you give him $2.99, he will give you what you paid for. If you didn't believe that, you wouldn't give him your money.

We always act according to our beliefs. That's why demonstrating the Word is an element in the law of faith.

God shows us in Scripture how important this is.

> *But be **doers** of the word, and not hearers only, deceiving yourselves. For if anyone is a hearer of the word and not a **doer**, he is like a man observing his natural face in a mirror; for he observes himself, goes away, and immediately forgets what kind of man he was. But he who looks into the perfect law of liberty and continues in it, and is not a forgetful hearer but a **doer** of the work, this one will be blessed in what he **does.***
>
> *James 1:22-25 (emphasis added)*

Many today are guilty of listening to the Word, reading the Word, and preaching the Word, but not doing the Word. It is one thing to say you believe in the miraculous; it is another to do it.

WE ALWAYS ACT ACCORDING TO OUR BELIEFS.

In one of our meetings, there was an old man who had a stroke. The entire right side of his body was paralyzed. His doctors said there was no hope. I preached that night on the power of God. I told the crowd that Jesus would heal them if they would put their faith in Him.

That paralyzed man could have heard the Word of God, agreed with it, and stayed in his wheelchair. But he didn't. He put his faith in action by doing the Word. He asked some people to help him up because he was going to walk. When those people helped him up and let go, he remained standing and started walking. His right arm was working too. It was a miracle.

He could have stayed in the wheelchair and said, "I believe, I believe, I believe," and never walked. The healing came when he put the Word into action.

Thus also faith by itself, if it does not have works, is dead.

But someone will say, "You have faith, and I have works." Show me your faith without your works, and I will show you my faith by my works. You believe that there is one God. You do well. Even the demons believe—and tremble! But do you want to know, O foolish man, that faith without works is dead? Was not Abraham our father justified by works when he offered Isaac his son on the altar? Do you see that faith was working together with his works, and by works faith was made perfect? And the Scripture was fulfilled which says, "Abraham believed God, and it was accounted to him for righteousness." And he was called the friend of God. You see then that a man is justified by works, and not by faith only.

Likewise, was not Rahab the harlot also justi-

*fied by works when she received the messengers and
sent them out another way?*

*For as the body without the spirit is dead, so
faith without works is dead also.*

James 2:17-26

We find in this passage that doing the
Word, or "works," is what quickens your faith.
Works makes a dead faith a living one. Works is
how we show our faith.

You can tell who has a living faith and who
doesn't. If you were dying of some incurable disease you will go and get prayer from someone who
has a living faith. Most likely you would not go to
the person who tells you to suffer for Jesus and die
at an early age. You would go to the person who
believes you can be healed and has a track record of
praying for people that are sick who receive miraculous healing.

A devout man in a denomination that
believes the time of miracles has passed found out
that his mother was dying of cancer and that the
doctors gave her no hope. He went to his pastor
and said I heard about a man of faith that believes
God still heals people. I am taking my mother to
him for prayer. His pastor told him that the man
was not a man of faith but just a good showman
and that Jesus did not still heal people.

Since the alternative of not going to see the
man of faith was death, he took his mother to him.

68

God reached down in his mercy and healed his mother of cancer through the man of faith. When the pastor found out about it, he said the devil must have done it.

The woman of cancer stood up and said, "All I know is that the man I saw prayed to Jesus Christ, declared Him as Lord, and proclaimed healing over my body. Instantly I was healed."

I receive lots of prayer requests from people who say their pastor doesn't believe in divine healing. They say that no one has ever received healing in their ministry.

> **WORKS MAKES A DEAD FAITH A LIVING ONE.**

So they contact my ministry, Holy Fire International, for prayer. They have seen or heard about the works of the ministry.

Are you able to say, "I will show you my faith by my works" like James did?

Nothing is stopping you from doing the Word. God wants you to act upon His Word.

I know several theologians who have memorized lots of Scripture, who study it and teach it, but have no practical application of their faith that helps hurting people. I am not saying that all theologians have dead faith, but if their theology does not help people, it is of little use. The Bible says we should turn away from people who have a form of godliness but deny its power (2 Timothy 3:5).

Putting our faith into action is so simple

many of us overlook it. We are waiting for God to act when, if fact, He has already acted and is waiting on us to act upon His Word. Although this may be simple, it is not always easy.

A pastor of a church I was attending asked if I would go with him to pray for a woman's mother who was having problems with her legs. The pastor told me he had never laid hands on someone to pray for their healing before.

We went to a small home, where we met a woman sitting on a couch and a man with a cane sitting in a chair. I asked the woman what problems she was experiencing. She replied, "I have pain in my legs and I can barely walk." I asked her if we could pray for her and she said yes.

I told her about how Jesus paid the price for her healing and that when we were done praying she would be healed. The man in the chair watched intently, but wanted no part of what was going on.

During the prayer the woman said she felt heat going down her spine and through her legs. At first she was scared and said, "What is this?" I told her it was the manifest power of God. She immediately got up and said, "I'm healed, I'm healed!" She started walking around the house, bending and stretching, trying to see if there was any pain. There wasn't. Hallelujah!

I asked the man in the chair if he would like us to pray for his healing. He said no. Even after seeing God heal in front of his very eyes, he still did not want to receive healing from God for himself.

At the next service at the local church, the woman who had been healed was there praising God. That is what it is about, taking the gospel of Jesus Christ to the hurting world.

If we want to be used to minister in the miraculous, we must put our faith into action by recognizing the Word, proclaiming the Word, and demonstrating the Word.

Demonstration of the Word is what separates Christianity from all other religions. No other religion has a God you can know personally, who lives inside you to do good by manifesting power, which demonstrates God's love for people. Anyone who has read Chapter 11 of Hebrews knows that people who have put this law of faith into action have seen God use them to manifest the miraculous in their lives. You will be able to see all four elements of faith in lives of anyone who is used by God to do the miraculous.

Jesus said:

Most assuredly, I say to you, he who believes in Me, the works that I do he will do also; and greater works than these he will do, because I go to My Father.
John 14:12

The Bible declares that:

For all the promises of God in Him are Yes, and

in Him Amen, to the glory of God through us. Now He who establishes us with you in Christ and has anointed us is God, who also has sealed us and given us the Spirit in our hearts as a guarantee.

2 Corinthians 1:20-22

Those three verses tell us that it is God's desire for us to operate in the manifest power of the Holy Spirit. All we have to do is be obedient to the Word of God and go out and do it.

CHAPTER NINE

RECEIVING THE RESULTS

Every time we recognize the Word, proclaim the Word, and demonstrate the Word, results will come. All the results belong to God for His glory. Jesus should receive all the glory and honor for every miraculous thing that happens as a result of the law of faith. All of the miracles that have taken place in my ministry are because of Jesus and what He has done for me. He alone is worthy.

If the goal of manifesting power is to glorify Jesus, we will never take the credit. If you have been at one of my meetings you will hear me say over and over, "Jesus has healed you," or "Jesus has done this miracle." In and of ourselves we can do nothing, but with Jesus Christ all things are possible (Philippians 4:13).

If you have done the first three elements in the law of faith, expect results, because they will happen. Often people give up just before the miracle.

There was a man at a recent crusade in India who was barely able to walk. He heard the Word of God and proclaimed it. Then he demonstrated the Word, putting it into action by standing up and starting to walk. He was in a lot of pain. He could have taken just one step and given up, but he didn't. The man said, "I will receive the results because the gospel is true." He kept walking, and every step got easier. Within a few minutes he was completely healed. Hallelujah!

This law of faith will work for you and your ministry. The Creator of the universe has established these biblical principles. Praise God! Dare to believe.

Have faith in God. For assuredly, I say to you, whoever says to this mountain, "Be removed and be cast into the sea," and does not doubt in his heart, but believes that those things he says will be done, he will have whatever he says. Therefore I say to you, whatever things you ask when you pray, believe that you receive them, and you will have them.

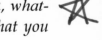

Mark 11:22-24

In this passage Jesus said, "Have faith in God." That means we must recognize the Word because faith comes by hearing the word of God (Romans 10:17). Jesus went on to say that whoever "says" or proclaims the Word of God with his mouth and believe in his heart he will have what he asks. If you believe in your heart, you will act like it by demonstrating the Word, and you will receive.

Two weeks ago a lady named Jill came to me for prayer. She said her friend was a member of a denomination that did not believe God still heals. Unfortunately her friend was sick and the doctors didn't know what was wrong with her. I agreed with Jill in prayer that her friend would be healed.

Last week Jill told me that when she asked for prayer she didn't think anything would happen. But the day we prayed, her friend was miraculously healed. The doctors were astounded and could not explain it. This gave Jill a perfect opportunity to witness to her friend of the miracle-working power of Jesus.

Jill asked God why this prayer was different. God told her that the man who prayed for her had faith and believed. I told her that nothing can stop her from seeing the same results every time she prays, because God is no respecter of persons. (Acts 10:34. 2 Chronicles 19:7, Romans 2:11)

CHAPTER TEN

SATAN'S GREAT DECEPTION

Satan is the king of deception. In this chapter we are going to look at how the enemy works and what tactics he uses to try to defeat you.

In the modern church there is a lot of debate over the devil and controversy about his abilities, especially when dealing with believers. We must realize what place he holds in the Christian's life and what our responsibility is to see the victory.

If you have been a Christian for any length of time, I am sure you have heard all kinds of doctrine concerning devils and demons. I have heard people teach doctrines based on an experience they had, twisting Scripture to fit the experience rather than fitting their experience to Scripture.

This issue is not as complicated as some

would make it. We will look to the Bible to understand who Satan is and what his goals are. We will
also see where we stand as Christians.

In Scripture Satan is called:
Wicked one (Matthew 13:19)
Enemy (Matthew 13:39)
Accuser of believers (Revelation 12:10)
Adversary (1 Peter 5:8)
Roaring lion (1 Peter 5:8)
Dragon (Revelation 20:2)
Serpent of old (Revelation 20:2)
Murderer (John 8:44)
Father of lies (John 8:44)
Tempter (Matthew 4:3)
Ruler of this world (John 14:30)
Corrupter of minds (2 Corinthians 11:3)

Because of Satan attributes, many are scared
of him, always looking over their shoulders, thinking the devil is going to get them. We need to realize the limits of the
power Satan has in
a believer's life. He
only has the power
we give him.

> **JESUS CHRIST HAS
> COMPLETE AUTHORITY
> OVER THE DEVIL AND
> HAS GIVEN THAT
> AUTHORITY TO EVERY
> BELIEVER.**

Satan is the
god of this world (2
Corinthians   4:4
KJV). However, as

Christians, we are not of the world (John 15:19), so we are not held captive by the god of this world. The Bible says: [Fixed fight?]

> You are of God, little children, and have overcome them, *because He who is in you is greater than he who is in the world.*
>
> 1 John 4:4

If you have accepted Jesus Christ as Lord and Savior of your life, then Jesus is in you. You can be assured that no weapon formed against you shall prosper.

> For this purpose the Son of God was manifested, that He might destroy the works of the devil.
>
> 1 John 3:8

> Having disarmed principalities and powers, He made a public spectacle of them, triumphing over them in it.
>
> Colossians 2:15

From these passages we see that Jesus has defeated the devil, and the devil has no power over Him. Praise God, that same Jesus lives in you and me! Jesus Christ has complete authority over the devil and has given that authority to every believer.

> *Behold, I give you the authority ... over all the*
> *power of the enemy.*

> Luke 10:19

We have complete authority ~~of~~ over all the power of the devil. Not just a little bit of author- ity, but all authority. We don't need to fear the devil. He fears us! Hallelujah!

So why are many Christians living defeat- ed lives? Why does it seem as if they are being kicked around by the devil? This is where Satan's great deception comes in. The devil knows he is defeated and that Jesus has given you authority over him, so he must resort to lying and deceiv- ing. Unfortunately, many Christians become vic- tims by believing in his lies.

Even in the beginning Satan deceived and lied to get man to sin.

> *Now the serpent was more cunning than any beast of the field which the Lord God had made. And he said to the woman, "Has God indeed said, 'You shall not eat of every tree of the garden'?"*

> *And the woman said to the serpent, "We may eat the fruit of the trees of the garden; but of the fruit of the tree which is in the midst of the garden, God has said, 'You shall not eat it, nor shall you touch it, lest you die.'"*

> *Then the serpent said to the woman, "You will not surely die. For God knows that in the day you eat*

of it your eyes will be opened, and you will be like God, knowing good and evil."

So when the woman saw that the tree was good for food, that it was pleasant to the eyes, and a tree desirable to make one wise, she took of its fruit and ate. She also gave to her husband with her, and he ate.

Genesis 3:1-6

Did Satan make Adam and Eve sin? No. What he did was pervert the word of God. Adam and Eve accepted the lie and sinned. If you are a child of God, Satan no longer has a hold on you, so he works to entice you into not believing what the Word says.

For example he might say:

"Did God really save you?"

"Your friend won't be healed just because you pray."

"You cannot command this storm to cease."

"God is using this terrible thing to teach you a lesson, so just suffer and endure."

Don't believe the lies. All Satan has is smoke and mirrors. You are an overcomer, more than victorious. You have been given all things that pertain to life. You're an ambassador for Christ. You have authority over all the power of the devil. Signs will follow you when you pray. You will do the works of Christ and even greater works!

So often we don't manifest the power of God because we have believed lies from the father of lies. All things are possible in Christ Jesus. We should put our trust in the Scripture rather than Satan's great deceptions.

If he can entice you to sin and put guilt and condemnation on you, he is happy, because when you are like that, you're not out manifesting the power of the Holy Spirit. God has given you power over the devil. All you have to do is recognize the Word, proclaim the Word, demonstrate the Word, and receive the results!

CHAPTER ELEVEN

HOLY SPIRIT

The Holy Spirit is vital in understanding the miraculous. You will not have the power of God in your life without the Holy Spirit. So it is important to understand His attributes.

Prior to the new covenant, the Holy Spirit would manifest for a specific purpose and time in a believer's life. The Holy Spirit did not indwell all believers until after Jesus established the new covenant. When Jesus put His blood on the mercy seat in the Holy of Holies in heaven as a perfect sacrifice for your sins and mine, we were justified and made righteous. Therefore we are now worthy to be vessels for the Holy Spirit because of Jesus' finished work on the cross. He is the one who baptizes us with the Holy Spirit.

John the Baptist said to his followers:

> *I indeed baptize you with water; but One mightier than I is coming, whose sandal strap I am not worthy to loose. He will baptize you with the Holy Spirit and fire.*
>
> *Luke 3:16*

> | YOU WILL RECEIVE POWER WHEN YOU RECEIVE THE HOLY SPIRIT. |

For John truly baptized with water, but you shall be baptized with the Holy Spirit.

Acts 1:5

What is the result of receiving the Holy Spirit? Power!

> *But you shall receive **power** when the Holy Spirit has come upon you; and you shall be witnesses to Me in Jerusalem, and in all Judea and Samaria, and to the end of the earth.*
>
> *Act 1:8 (emphasis added)*

You will receive power when you receive the Holy Spirit. That power is given for you to be His witness to everyone. Not for selfish gain, personal recognition, or monetary reward. It is for the sole purpose of glorifying Jesus Christ, because the Holy Spirit bears witness to Christ.

On the day of Pentecost, the Holy Spirit

came upon 120 people and they spoke in tongues. Peter preached boldly to thousands who came to a saving knowledge of Jesus. Peter and John ministered healing to a paralytic at the Gate Beautiful. That promise of power was not just for the apostles; it is also for us today.

> *Then Peter said to them, "Repent, and let every one of you be baptized in the name of Jesus Christ for the remission of sins; and you shall receive the gift of the Holy Spirit. For the promise is to you and to your children, and to all who are afar off, as many as the Lord our God will call."*

Acts 2:38-39

There are a lot of preachers today who will not minister until they feel a certain way. They lead large groups of people in worship but will not pray until they feel the presence of the Holy Spirit. While they minister with success, I would submit to you that how you feel does not matter. If you are in a heathen nation with an

> **YOU DON'T KNOW YOU HAVE THE POWER UNTIL YOU USE IT.**

audience full of pagans who curse you with their every breath, you may be waiting a long time until the atmosphere seems right to you. Trust me, I know; I've been there. God's power is not dependent upon your feelings. If you are in Christ and full of the Holy Spirit, you have the power.

You don't know you have the power until you use it. This is one of the most difficult princi-ples to understand, but it makes sense if you think about it. If you are waiting until God manifests power in your life, you will be waiting a long time. God will manifest power when you use it.

> **THE POWER COMES BECAUSE OF WHO JESUS IS AND WHAT HE HAS DONE, NOT BECAUSE OF HOW WE FEEL.**

A man came to me once and told me he was waiting for God to give him the gift of healing. I asked him how many sick people he had prayed for. He told me he had not prayed for anyone because he was waiting for God to give him the power. I told him he had the power, and God was waiting on him to use it. First he had to understand the law of faith, which requires understanding the Word and putting it into action.

Sitting around waiting for faith to do the miraculous will only bring boredom. Faith comes by hearing the Word of God. Then God uses us to minister the miraculous.

Some of the greatest miracles I have seen in my ministry came when I felt nothing. On a recent trip I arrived in the town where I was invited to speak a day early. I knew I would be exhausted from staying awake for several days of travel and

86

jet leg. When I got to the parking lot of the airport, I was informed that I had to speak in a couple of hours because of a schedule change. I was prepared for the message but was barely awake and physically exhausted. My message was short, and when I finished I prayed a prayer for healing. I didn't feel a great move of the Holy Spirit. There were no goose bumps, no one was shouting or falling under the power. But suddenly the deaf received hearing and the lame started walking. It was miraculous. The power of God manifested, to the amazement of everyone.

The power comes because of who Jesus is and what He has done, not because of how we feel.

A few months ago I was preaching on a Sunday morning in a traditional church where I had preached the year before. At that time, the people had been extremely reserved and dry.

When I returned, I felt the presence of the Holy Spirit quite strongly. As I started my message, I could barely contain my enthusiasm. I knew God was going to do something big in that church. The power was so strong people started falling out of their pews under the power of the Holy Spirit during my message.

I stopped and prayed. Almost no one in attendance could stand on his feet because of the presence of God. There was wailing and repentance.

This was an unusual manifestation in this

traditional church. Even though I did not preach a salvation message, people came forward asking how they could know this Jesus.

I have given you these examples so you will realize that we cannot put the Holy Spirit in a box. We cannot say there is only one way to minister as it relates to our human feelings and understanding. But no matter how we minister, it should always bring glory to Jesus Christ.

CHAPTER

TWELVE

DISCOVER YOUR VALUE

You have great value to the kingdom of God. God has chosen you and trusted you to fulfill His plan. Many of us say we put our trust in God, but do you realize that God has chosen to put His trust in you?

We have been chosen to represent Jesus and proclaim the gospel. God has chosen people to do that. In Scripture we are commanded to preach the gospel.

Many in the body of Christ see themselves as worthless sinners, no good and of no value. Jesus said you have great value. You had great value even before you received Christ as Lord and Savior.

> *God demonstrates His own love toward us, in that while we were still sinners, Christ died for us.*
>
> *Romans 5:8*

If we say we have no value, then Christ died for nothing. God loves you and wants you to understand how important you are. He wants you to succeed and not fail. He is not waiting for you to make a mistake so He can squash you like a bug. Jesus didn't come to condemn you but to save you.

> *Whoever believes in Him should not perish but have eternal life. For God so loved the world that He gave His only begotten Son, that whoever believes in Him should not perish but have everlasting life. For God did not send His Son into the world to condemn the world, but that the world through Him might be saved.*
>
> *John 3:15-17*

IF WE SAY WE HAVE NO VALUE, THEN CHRIST DIED FOR NOTHING.

If you are a Christian, when God looks at you He sees the blood of Jesus. You are sinless in His sight. You are His child and He only wants the best for you. God loves you so much that He sacrificed His Son for your life. You have tremendous value and God has a desire to use you for His kingdom.

90

For you made us only a little lower than God, and you crowned us with glory and honor.

You put us in charge of everything you made, giving us authority over all things.

Psalm 8:5–6 NLT.

If God declares us righteous and justified because of Christ, who are we to say that we are not. We need to change our mentality about who we are and what value we have. If we see ourselves the way God sees us, we will pray in boldness and faith, which will bring about power.

Many confuse boldness and assuredness with pride. Pride is when we put ourselves above others and receive glory and honor for ourselves. Boldness and assuredness is when we know who we are in Christ and speak forth His Word and expect it to happen for the glory of God. We need to speak out and say, "When I pray for you, you will be healed." That is not pride but assurance in the Word of God, knowing we can do what the Word says we can do and that God is who He says He is.

 Just as people confuse pride with boldness, they also confuse humility with timidity. Many think that if you are holy, you will be a timid little mouse, almost afraid to speak. That is not humility. Humility is submitting yourself to the will of God and giving Him all the glory and honor for every-

91

thing in your life.

If someone asks you, "Who do you think you are that you would be able to command this storm to cease?" you can tell that person you are a child of God and that God has given you authority on this earth and you will give Jesus all the glory and honor. Be bold in the power of the Holy Spirit, because God loves you and trusts you to do His will.

Not only do children of God have value, everyone does. It doesn't matter who they are or what country they are in. It doesn't matter how much money they have or how many sins they have committed. God loves them and wishes that none would perish. This motivates me to witness to all people, no matter who they are, because they have value and God has trusted me with the gospel. People need what we have. There is nothing that is impossible with Jesus!

"Their sins and their lawless deeds I will remember no more." Now where there is remission of these, there is no longer an offering for sin.

Therefore, brethren, having boldness to enter the Holiest by the blood of Jesus, by a new and living way which He consecrated for us, through the veil, that is, His flesh, and having a High Priest over the house of God, let us draw near with a true heart in full assurance of faith, having our hearts sprinkled from an evil conscience and our bodies washed with pure water. Let us hold fast the confession of our hope without wavering, for He who promised is faithful. And let us consider one another in order to stir up love and good works, not forsaking the assembling of ourselves together, as is the manner of some, but exhorting one another, and so much the more as you see the Day approaching.

Hebrews 10:17-25

We serve a faithful God. He does not remember our past deeds. He gives us value. The Bible tells us that we should have boldness because we have a new and living way that Jesus consecrated for us.

CHAPTER THIRTEEN

PRACTICAL APPLICATION

Okay. You have grasped the principles and you're seeing yourself as God sees you. Now what? It is time to apply that knowledge and make the most of every opportunity.

You do not need to be an evangelist or pastor to apply the knowledge you have gained. This is for every believer. Some have said, "I am a homemaker. What can I do?" Or, "I am not a theologian; I have not reached the level necessary for practical application." They could not be further from the truth. You are ready if you understand the simple points brought out in this book.

I know a man named Bill who is not a preacher, teacher, or church leader. He has a full-time job and attends weekly services at his local church. One day, while Bill was at a gas station, he was going inside to pay for his gas when he overheard a man telling his friend he had a severe pain in his back.

Bill interrupted and asked the man if it would be okay if he prayed for him. The man said yes, probably not realizing that Bill was going to pray right then and there. Bill immediately started praying a short prayer and touched the man's back. The man respectfully said thanks and went into the gas station.

Bill paid for his gas, then went out to fill his tank. After a few minutes the man Bill had prayed for came up to him and asked if he was an angel. "All the pain is gone," he said.

"I'm no angel," Bill replied. "I am a Christian man, and God's Word says I can pray for you and you will be healed.

NOTHING CAN STOP THE POWER OF THE HOLY SPIRIT IN YOU WHEN YOU PRAY AND BELIEVE.

This gave Bill an opportunity to witness to this man about the love of Jesus and tell him about the salvation Jesus offers. Praise God! If every Christian would manifest the Lord's power like Bill did, this world would drastically change.

You have lots of opportunities to minister regardless of your occupation, financial status, or schedule. Think about every time you have run into someone who needed a touch from the Lord or an unbeliever who was hurting. You can minister to these people in boldness and assuredness because you are a child of God who understands the law of faith. Nothing can stop the power of the Holy Spirit in you when you pray and believe.

At the end of the week, think about how many people you have come in contact with. How many of them had a need? How many were unsaved? You and I have the answers to life's most difficult questions. We have the answer to sickness, depression, and despair. We know the cure for every incurable disease.

The apostle Paul said:

> YOU HAVE WHAT THIS WORLD NEEDS, AND ALL YOU HAVE TO DO IS BELIEVE YOU HAVE IT AND GIVE IT AWAY.

Grace and peace be multiplied to you in the knowledge of God and of Jesus our Lord, as His divine power has given to us all things that pertain to life and godliness, through the knowledge of Him who called us by glory and virtue, by which have been given to us exceedingly great and precious promises, that through these you may be partakers of the divine nature.

2 Peter 1: 2-4

You have been given all things that pertain to life and godliness. That is powerful. My friend, you have what this world needs, and all you have to do is believe you have it and give it away. Unlimited ministry abounds for every believer, including you, and unlimited success abounds for every believer, including you.

Many people are waiting on a call or divine intervention before they will minister the Word of God in their daily lives. God has already equipped you and given you the call to help all those in need by ministering His power. It is in His Word.

CHAPTER FOURTEEN

COMMON OBJECTIONS

There are some leaders in the church today who object to manifesting the power of the Holy Spirit through believers in Jesus Christ. Because of these objections, many do not believe that we Christians are called to do the miraculous.

In this chapter I would like to look at these objections and show you what the Word of God says about them. We will also look at some reasons people have objections.

Abuse and Misuse

The reason many object to the manifest power of God in the believer is the misuse and abuse of some who proclaim they are doing the

99

miraculous when they are really operating in the flesh. This is particularly prevalent with television evangelists.

I am not saying that everyone on television who claims God is using them in the miraculous is bad. But some are turning people away. For example, they may say, "Send me your seed (money) and receive your miracle harvest (manifest power)." Ministers who do this must have ripped the following passage out of their Bibles.

And when Simon saw that through the laying on of the apostles' hands the Holy Spirit was given, he offered them money, saying, "Give me this power also, that anyone on whom I lay hands may receive the Holy Spirit."

But Peter said to him, "Your money perish with you, because you thought that the gift of God could be purchased with money! You have neither part nor portion in this matter, for your heart is not right in the sight of God. Repent therefore of this your wickedness, and pray God if perhaps the thought of your heart may be forgiven you. For I see that you are poisoned by bitterness and bound by iniquity."

Acts 8:18-23

Never give money to a ministry that claims to sell the anointing, no matter what form it is in. Don't pay for an anointed prayer cloth. God tells us in Matthew 10:7-8 that we have received the power freely and freely we should give it. Just because some ministers are acting in the flesh, that shouldn't stop us from being biblical and producing real results. The devil always tries to imitate the real thing.

Yes, there is abuse and misuse of ministry today, but don't lump everyone who is doing the miraculous work of Christ into that category. This is one of the major reasons some people search for alternate answers that oppose believers being used to manifest power.

> **NEVER GIVE MONEY TO A MINISTRY THAT CLAIMS TO SELL THE ANOINTING, NO MATTER WHAT FORM IT IS IN.**

Anyone who spends twenty-eight minutes of their thirty-minute evangelistic show begging you for money and telling you should trust God to meet your financial needs should look in the mirror and listen to their own advice.

The other reason leaders in the church look for objections to the manifest power of God is control. If everyone has the anointing and is used powerfully by God, then some leaders may feel their self-worth is being attacked and they won't be able to stay on their pedestal. If they are autocratic leaders and have placed themselves above you spiritually, they can control you. I submit to you that every believer has the same authority and

power in Christ because God is no respecter of per- *11*
sons.   *Not partial*

We do need accountability in the local
church. But I do not support leaders who don't
encourage all believers to be used by God. Many
speak against individuals manifesting power
because of their own lack of faith. The Bible says
that such people have a form of godliness but deny
its power and that we should turn away from them
(2 Timothy 3:5).

Present-day Power

Many have said that miracles ceased with
the apostles or the first century. Let's look at this
issue. I have already shown you how Stephen was
used to do great signs and wonders among the people (Acts 6). The 120 in the upper room (Acts 2) and
the seventy disciples also went out and ministered
in power (Matthew 10:1-20).

Many try to show some separations from
A.D. 100 to the present, but we are all part of the
same covenant, the covenant we have with the
Father because of Jesus Christ. In the New
Testament church, all who believe will be used in
power (John 14:12).

In the original Greek the book of Acts was
titled *praxeis*, which simply means "acts." The
same acts that are recorded in this book of the Bible
have continued over the last 2000 years. We are still

in the church age doing acts.

Below is just a short list of those who either were used in the manifest power of God or wrote about people of their time who were used.

Justin Martyr (A.D. 100—65)
Iraneaus (A.D. 125–200)
Tertullian (A.D. 160–240)
Origen (A.D. 185–284)
Antony (A.D. 251–358)
Pachomius (A.D. 295–373)
Hilarion (A.D. 305–385)
Ambrose (A.D. 340–397)
Jerome (A.D. 347–420)
Benedict (A.D. 480–547)
Gregory (A.D. 540–604)
Ansgar (A.D. 800–865)
Bernard (A.D. 1090–1153)
Doninic (A.D. 1170–1221)
Peter Waldo (A.D. 1217
Martin Luther (A.D. 1483–1546)
George Fox (A.D. 1624–1691)
John Wesley (A.D. 1703–1791)
Jonathan Edwards (early 1700s)
George Whitfield (A.D. 1714–1770)
Edward Irving (A.D. 1792–1834)
Charles Finney (A.D. 1792–1873)
A. J. Gordon (A.D. 1836–1895)
Ruben Torrey (A.D. 1856–1928)

This list shows just a fraction of the people recorded in history that God used to work miracles since the apostles. Anyone who thinks that miracles died with the first century would have to rewrite a lot of history. You can add your name to that list when you step out in the manifest power of God.

Divine Healing

There are objections to divine healing because of topics like Paul's thorn in the flesh, Paul's eyesight, and God's will. We will look at each of these briefly and see what the Bible says about them.

Thorn in the Flesh

The passage in the Bible about Paul's thorn in the flesh reads:

And lest I should be exalted above measure by the abundance of the revelations, a thorn in the flesh was given to me, a messenger of Satan to buffet me, lest I be exalted above measure. Concerning this thing I pleaded with the Lord three times that it might depart from me. And He said to me, "My grace is sufficient for you, for My strength is made perfect in weakness."

2 Corinthians 12:7-9

The term "thorn in the flesh" was used in the Old Testaments, but not to indicate sickness.

But if you fail to drive out the people who live in the land, those who remain will be like splinters in your eyes and thorns in your sides. They will harass you in the land where you live.

Numbers 33:55 (NLT)

Know for certain that the Lord your God will no longer drive out these nations from before you. But they shall be snares and traps to you, and scourges on your sides and thorns in your eyes, until you perish from this good land which the Lord your God has given you.

Joshua 23:13

In these passages the thorns in the flesh were the inhabitants of the land, not a physical infirmity or an actual thorn piercing the flesh. Paul was a great scholar of the Old Testament, so he would have understood the term.

He even told us what the thorn was in 2 Corinthians 12:7. "A thorn in the flesh was given to me, a messenger of Satan to buffet me, lest I be exalted above measure." The thorn was a messenger of Satan. The Greek word used here for messenger appears 188 times in the Bible, and it never refers to disease. *Acts 20:23 Acts 28:30-31*

This thorn was given to Paul so he wouldn't be exalted above measure because of his abundance of revelation. I don't know too many people today who fall into that category.

Paul's Eyesight

Many have claimed that Paul's thorn in the flesh was being almost blind, based on this Scripture:

See with what large letters I have written to you with my own hand!

Galatians 6:11

A simple word study will clear up this issue. The word *large* in this Scripture is the Greek word *payleekos*, which refers to a quantitative form or "how much" of something. Paul is referring here to the length of the letter, not the size of the letters it contained. If he were talking about the size of the letters he would have used the Greek word *megas*, which means "big."

Paul is essentially saying, "Look at how long this letter is that I have written to you with my own handwriting." It was not his custom to do his own writing at that time. So he isn't describing some type of disease of the eye.

God's Will

This is one of the biggest excuses used when

people pray and nothing happens. That is why it is a common objection of the miraculous.

Just as it is God's will that all be saved (2 Peter 3:9), it is God's will for all to be healed (1 Peter 2:24). Healing was provided for by the same sacrifice. Jesus healed *everyone* who came to him. (See Mark 1:40–42, Matthew 10:1; 12:25; 14:14; 34:36; Luke 16:17–19) The Bible makes it clear that He took on our sickness.

That evening many demon-possessed people were brought to Jesus. All the spirits fled when he commanded them to leave; and he healed all the sick. This fulfilled the word of the Lord through Isaiah, who said, "He took our sickness and removed our diseases."

Matthew 8:16-17 (NLT)

Praise God, Jesus is the same yesterday, today, and forever (Hebrews 13:8). We can be certain that when we come to God in faith, He is faithful to answer.

This section is not intended to fully outline all the aspects of divine healing, but to show you a few of the common objections to it. No matter what the argument, we should go to Scripture to find the answers. God will reveal His truth to us through the power of the Holy Spirit.

CHAPTER FIFTEEN

WHAT IT MEANS TO BE A CHRISTIAN

Many people today claim to be Christians. But are they really? Are you? In this chapter I will go over God's plan of salvation.

Perhaps you have been deceived into thinking that there are multiple ways to heaven. There are a lot of mislead people who believe that it doesn't matter what religion we have. They believe if they are good enough they will go to heaven. The Bible is very clear on how to get to heaven and there is only one way!

First we must realize our need. None of us are good enough to fulfill the law of the old covenant. None of us has lived a sinless life. The Bible declares *all have sinned and fall short of the glory of God* (Romans 3:23).

109

Romans 6:23 says *the wages of sin is death*. Death is the punishment for sin.

But God loves us so much that He took the punishment for our sins upon Himself so that we could be free. Hallelujah! The Bible says, *"God demonstrates His own love toward us, in that while we were still sinners, Christ died for us" (Romans 5:8)*. God was not willing that any should perish, but that all should have life through His perfect sacrifice (II Peter 3:9).

Jesus solved the problem of your death penalty for your sin because *"the gift of God is eternal life in Christ Jesus our Lord" (Romans 6:23)*. Salvation is a free gift; all you have to do is accept it.

Many times people come to me and say, "I can't believe how simple this is, but I feel completely free and at peace now." Praise God!

Here are five steps you can do right now to receive Jesus and know that you are a true Christian.

1. Realize that you have sinned.

First John 1:8 says, *"If we say that we have no sin , we deceive ourselves."* Romans 3:23 say, *"All have sinned and fall short of the glory of God."*

2. Repent and confess of your sins.

John said, *"If we confess our sins, He is faithful and just to forgive us our sins, and to cleanse us from all unrighteousness"* (1 John 1:9). If you truly repent of your sins, you will turn from them and forsake them.

3. Consecrate your life to Christ.

When you have faith in Jesus, you will apply the law of faith. You will demonstrate your faith by your actions. You will try to live a life worthy of the sacrifice God has given.

4. Believe that God saves you by His grace.

"For by grace you have been saved through faith, and that not of yourselves; it is the gift of God, not of works, lest anyone should boast." (Ephesians 2:8-9) You didn't earn your salvation. It is a gift of God. Once you have received that gift, you will produce good works (James 2:17-20).

5. Pray the salvation prayer.

Pray this out loud:

Lord, I come to You in prayer, thanking You that You loved me so much that You gave Your Son, Jesus Christ, as a sacrifice for my sin. I acknowledge that I have sinned against You and that my sins have separated me from You. I repent and ask that You forgive me of all my sins. Cleanse me from all guilt. I confess that Jesus Christ is Lord, and I believe He was raised from the dead. I thank You that Your blood has washed all my sins away. I know that I am saved! Lead, guide, and direct all my ways. In Jesus' name I pray. Amen.

It is that simple.

If you prayed that prayer, we would love to hear from you and rejoice with you.

CHAPTER SIXTEEN

MINISTRY AND CONTACT INFORMATION

We travel all over the world speaking in churches, fields, hospitals, schools, youth events, conferences, seminars, colleges and seminaries. My wife is also an International Women's Speaker and singer.

Our sole purpose is to share the love of Jesus to the world. We go and minister regardless of the size, place or money, because it is all about Jesus and not about what we can get for our ministry.

We would love for you to contact our ministry if this book has blessed you in any way especially if you prayed the prayer to except Jesus into your life as Lord and Savior.

Evangelist Ed Hensel
Holy Fire International, Inc.
P.O. Box 5192
Oak Ridge, TN 37831-5192

Web site: www.edhensel.org
E-Mail address: power@edhensel.org

To contact us about Ministry Scheduling:
Email: Schedule@edhensel.org

ISBN 0-9745212-0-5

9 780974 521206

90000